John Elway

By
T. J. Andersen

CRESTWOOD HOUSE

Mankato, Minnesota
U.S.A.

LIBRARY OF CONGRESS CATALOGING IN PUBLICATION DATA

Andersen, T.J.
    John Elway
    SUMMARY: Traces the life and career of the quarterback who led the Denver Broncos in three of the four best seasons in their history, between 1984 and 1986.
    1. Elway, John, 1960-   —Juvenile literature.   2. Football players—United States—Biography—Juvenile literature.   3. Denver Broncos (Football team)—Juvenile literature.   [1. Elway, John, 1960-   .   2. Football players.] I. Title. II. Series. III. Series: Sports close-ups.
GV939.E48A53   1988   796.332'092'4—dc19   [B]   [92]   87-27430
ISBN 0-89686-367-0

International Standard Book Number:	Library of Congress Catalog Card Number:
0-89686-367-0	87-27430

PHOTO CREDITS

Cover: Focus West: (Dave Black)
Focus West: (D. Strohmeyer) 32
Sports Illustrated: (Carl Iwasaki) 8, 43; (Damien Strohmeyer) 18-19, 44-45; (Andy Havt) 30-31, 47; (Rich Clarkson) 46
UPI/Bettmann News Photos: 14-15; (Mike Hill) 10; (Joe Marquette) 16; (Ken Levine) 29; (J. David Ake) 38-39
Focus on Sports: 4, 7, 23, 25, 26, 35, 36, 37; (Rob Brown) 20-21
AP/Wide World Photos: (Lennox McLendon) 41

Produced by Carnival Enterprises.

Box 3427, Mankato, MN, U.S.A. 56002

TABLE OF CONTENTS

John Elway is a new breed of quarterback.

A NEW BREED

John Albert Elway, the starting quarterback for the Denver Broncos, began his NFL career in 1983. During that year, there were only two rookie quarterbacks who became regular starters. The other was Dan Marino of the Miami Dolphins.

As a rookie, John was compared to many great quarterbacks in NFL history. A teammate said that Elway had legs like Fran Tarkenton, the Minnesota Viking quarterback during the 1970's. Others have compared John to Terry Bradshaw, the famous Pittsburgh Steeler quarterback. One sportscaster called John a "Namath with knees." As quarterback for the New York Jets, Joe Namath was intelligent, talented, and a flashy player. But his weak knees kept him out of play for whole seasons at a time. Namath spent as much time recuperating from knee operations as he did running and passing on the field.

A Bronco coach thought the same thing about John. "He's the best right out of college since Joe Namath," he said. Almost everyone else—fans and experts alike— agreed with him.

"I thought Joe Namath got a lot of press and publicity when he was a rookie, but it was nothing in comparison with what Elway's getting," said a Bronco spokesman, before the 1983 season. During all of this time, there were some people who were *not* comparing John to winning veteran quarterbacks. In fact, they were saying just the opposite. They called John Elway "a new breed" and "one of a kind." To them, he was completely different from any other quarterback, and he had everything going for him.

While the Broncos were still in training camp, a Denver newspaper began carrying a daily column, "The Elway Watch." In it, they ran every piece of news about John Elway they could find. Soon John Elway T-shirts began to appear. And all of this was happening *before* his first pro season had even started!

For John, all this attention was a burden as well as a blessing. It would be hard for anyone to live up to the expectations that the football world had placed on him.

GROWING UP

John, along with his twin sister, Jana, was born in Port Angeles, Washington, on June 28, 1960. Their sister, Lee Ann, had been born a year and a half earlier. John's dad was a football coach, and he looked forward to sharing football and other sports with his new son.

From the beginning, it was obvious that John was a natural athlete. One story his family loves to tell was about John's learning to switch hit the first time he picked up a bat. He could bat right-handed or left-handed—as a toddler!

His football career began in elementary school. In fifth grade, he was a running back. "That's what I wanted to be," he recalls. "I was always the fastest kid in my class. Then in the seventh grade I started growing and my speed went. That's when I became a quarterback."

Control, sharp eyes, and confidence make a good quarterback.

John with his favorite coach, his father Jack.

While John was growing up, the family moved several times—from Port Angeles to Montana, and then back to the state of Washington. They moved again to southern California, where John's father, Jack Elway, was hired as head coach at Cal State-Northridge, near Los Angeles.

Before the family chose which neighborhood they would live in, John's father made a study of all the local high school football coaches. When he found the one he thought could teach his son the most, the family bought a house in that school district.

The coach was Jack Neumier, and the high school was in Granada Hills. Neumier tutored John in the passing game. In high school, John was learning to pass and read defenses as well as most college quarterbacks.

At Granada Hills High School, John played both baseball and football. He was equally good at both sports. As a senior, he led the baseball team to the Los Angeles City Championship with a .491 batting average. His high school football record was so impressive that his jersey, number 11, was retired when he graduated. John worked hard in school, too. He managed to keep a grade point average of 3.8.

Because of his record, many college recruiters were talking to John about playing college football. One of these was his father, who was now head coach at San Jose State. Another recruiter was Rod Dowhower, a former Bronco assistant coach who had become head coach at Stanford University in Palo Alto, California.

John's baseball performance had also attracted the attention of scouts. The Kansas City Royals, a pro baseball club, selected him in the 1979 summer draft. By then, though, John had already signed a letter of intent with Stanford.

"JUST ONE OF THE GUYS"

The summer before his freshman year at Stanford, John began practicing with the team. Several former Stanford quarterbacks—including Steve Dils and Jim Plunkett—had come back to work out with the team, even though they were now playing in the pros.

One day, Coach Dowhower came back into the office from the field. He was shaking his head. He said about John, "You can't believe this kid. He's already better than all those guys."

Also during his freshman year, John met Janet Buchan, a freshman from Tacoma, Washington. She was also a fine athlete, setting several swimming records while still in high school. John described Janet as "a happy-go-lucky girl whom everybody likes to be around."

Playing for Stanford.

Although Stanford fans were eager to see John start during his freshman year, the coach kept him on the sidelines. But by sophomore year, the starting spot as quarterback was his. John compiled amazing statistics and was the first sophomore All-American in 18 years.

John's fame on the field increased steadily, but he did not let it affect his personal life. "Football's great," he said in college. "I love to play football. I think about football a lot, but I leave it on the field. When I'm not on the field, I'm just one of the guys."

His idea of a good time was to sit around the fraternity house with his friends, watching old shows on TV. Or, for a change, they might all go to a nearby arcade to play video games.

John did not forget that he was also at Stanford to get a college education. He was one of the few number-one picks in the NFL draft to graduate on time with his class. John majored in economics, and Janet, who also graduated in 1983, majored in sociology. That same spring, they announced their engagement.

FOOTBALL OR BASEBALL?

According to the rules of the National Football League, the team in last place at the end of a season gets first choice of new players in the following year's draft. In 1983, the year John was a senior at Stanford, this consolation prize went to the Baltimore Colts. They had not won a game all season.

For three months, John had been making his wishes known. He did not want to play for Baltimore. Instead, he wanted to be picked by a West Coast NFL team. He had grown up on the West Coast, he had gone to college on the West Coast, and his family still lived there.

During the summer of 1982, before his senior year at Stanford, John had signed a $150,000 contract with the New York Yankees to play six weeks of minor league baseball in Oneonta, New York. His position was outfield, and his batting average during that time was .318.

Although his experience in Class A baseball didn't prove that he could succeed in the major leagues, the New York Yankees were interested in him. And John was interested in them — *if* he was not picked by an NFL team he wanted to play for.

The Colts could have traded their pick to the San Diego Chargers, the Seattle Seahawks, or the Los Angeles Raiders — all teams on the West Coast. Instead, Baltimore went ahead and picked John as their number-one draft choice. John, his agent, and his father immediately called a press conference. "Right now, it looks like I'll be playing baseball with the Yankees," said John. By rejecting the Colts' offer, John became the first number-one draft pick ever to challenge the draft system.

John played Class A (minor league) ball for the Yankees.

The new Denver Bronco quarterback.

SIGNING WITH THE BRONCOS

On May 2, after two weeks of discussion, the Colts finally traded their rights to John to the Denver Broncos. In return for Elway, the Broncos gave the Colts their rights to two future draft picks and their backup quarterback.

John received a five-year, $5 million contract. He became the highest-paid rookie in the NFL and the Broncos' highest-paid player. Edgar Kaiser, owner of the Denver Broncos at that time, didn't seem to mind the price he paid for John. "I don't believe Elway was *outrageously* expensive, just expensive," joked Kaiser. "The worst thing that can happen is maybe he won't turn out to be better than Joe Namath."

Besides a five-year contract to play pro football, John also got something else—publicity. By the time the contract was signed, everyone who followed football recognized his name.

ELWAYMANIA

From the moment that John signed with Denver, Bronco fans developed a serious case of Elwaymania. Sportswriters and reporters for newspapers and television flooded the Bronco training camp.

Seven trailers for TV and radio were parked alongside

Meeting the press is part of the job.

the practice field. In three of the trailers, TV sportscasters hosted daily sports talk shows that lasted three to four hours each! The subject of conversation was Elway, Elway, Elway.

Meanwhile, at the Bronco ticket office, calls were pouring in. The Broncos, who had been sold out for every

regular-season game since 1970, already had a long waiting
list. Now the list was even longer. The Broncomaniacs, as
the fans were called, had stuck by their team through some
losing seasons. Now that they finally had an exciting young
quarterback and a shot at success, Broncomaniacs were
going wild!

THE FIRST GAME

In his first appearance on an NFL field, John showed he would not disappoint his fans. The Broncos were playing a mid-August exhibition game against the Seattle Seahawks, and Coach Dan Reeves put John in at the

John never gives up, even under pressure.

beginning of the second half. The Broncos were trailing Seattle 7-3. Just 4 minutes and 22 seconds into the second half, all that changed.

In his first 10 plays as a pro, John marched the Broncos 75 yards into the Seattle end zone for the winning touchdown. It was raining the whole time, but John still

managed to complete five of six passes. The fans were beside themselves, and the noise from the stands was deafening. By the end of the game, Elway had completed 8 of 17 passes, with only one interception.

After the game, reporters crowded around John in the locker room. He was modest about his own performance and praised his teammates. "I've got a long way to go, and a lot to learn," he said.

THE RISK OF A ROOKIE QUARTERBACK

Quarterbacks have been called "the only officers among football players." When the team is on the field, the quarterback is in command. The other team members are soldiers. Quarterbacks meet with the coaching staff every day to plot strategies against the next week's team. On a winning team, quarterbacks get the glory. On a losing team, they must take the blame.

Because quarterbacks are so important to the team, coaches have always felt that they needed lots of time to study the plays before starting a game. So instead of playing, rookie quarterbacks sit on the bench—sometimes for years—watching and learning.

But in Denver, the situation was different. The Bronco starting quarterback was Steve DeBerg. He had come to the Broncos from San Francisco and had been playing in Denver for two seasons. His performance seemed to be slipping.

On the other hand, Elway had pro-style playing experience in college. His footwork was so good that people compared it to that of a middleweight boxer. And his throwing arm was fantastic. "He's got such a quick release," said Coach Reeves.

Equally important, John had joined a team that was rebuilding. The Broncos were looking for instant leadership. It was hard to find reasons *not* to start John in his first year.

A quarterback needs a quick release.

ROOKIE YEAR

"The hardest thing facing a first-round pick quarterback," said one head coach, "is the level of expectation put on him by everyone, combined with the great demands of his job and the short time he has to learn it."

For John, what he didn't know in his first year was more important than what he did know. Coach Reeves was an ex-Dallas Cowboy offensive assistant, and his current Bronco playbook was full of plays as complicated as the ones used by Dallas.

For the first five weeks of the season, the Denver coach started John. But John frequently ran into trouble. "John's biggest problem," Reeves said, "was I'd send in a play and then he'd have to call the formation. It was all strange to him, like a foreign language. He had to call it, get up to the line and get it off, all in 30 seconds. He didn't have time to look at the defense. Everything was a blur."

Reeves finally benched John for four weeks in the late fall. At the same time, the coach admitted that he had expected Elway to learn too much too soon.

It was in a November game with the Seahawks that John unexpectedly returned to the lineup. Near the end of the third quarter, starting quarterback Steve DeBerg injured his shoulder. The Broncos were trailing 20-9. Elway led the Broncos in a rally. Although it was too late to reverse the outcome and the Seahawks won 27-19, John showed that his time on the bench had not been wasted.

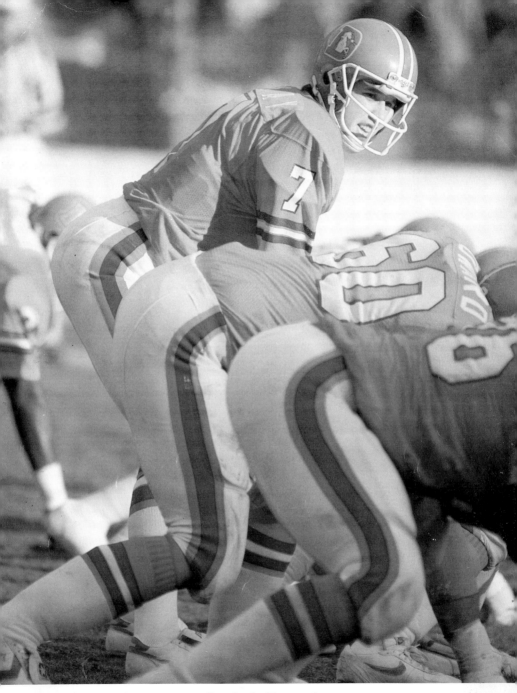

As a rookie, John learned to get off a play in 30 seconds.

In the pocket, Elway is cool.

John shared the rest of the '83 season with DeBerg, whose shoulder separation kept him on the bench for five weeks. DeBerg played in 10 games, while Elway played in 11.

In December, John had two outstanding games. Against Cleveland, he completed 16 of 24 passes for 284 total yards and two touchdowns against the Browns. The next week against Baltimore he brought Denver back from 19-0, with three fourth-quarter touchdown passes. The Broncos snatched the win from the Colts 21-19. That victory clinched a playoff spot for the Broncos.

At the end of season play, John had logged 123 completions in 259 passing attempts (47.5%) gaining 1,663 yards. In rushing, his average was 5.2 yards. He threw 7 touchdown passes and had 14 passes intercepted.

His statistics were not impressive, but they weren't that much worse than the statistics of some other quarterbacks. But for someone who was expected to put in a perfect first year, John's performance fell far short. Although he never completely lost his confidence, he had some frustrating times. Janet was living in Seattle—they were planning to get married after his rookie year—and he often called her to discuss his problems.

Looking back, Janet knows that she couldn't have helped him, even if she had been in Denver. "He was going to have to go through what he did by himself." As planned, they were married after the end of John's first season with the Broncos.

PRACTICE MAKES PERFECT

In his second season, John became a permanent starter for the Broncos. Steve DeBerg was traded by the Broncos to the Tampa Bay Buccaneers.

In the three seasons since he has been Denver's regular starting quarterback, John has led the Broncos to 34 regular season wins, more than any NFL quarterback except for the Miami Dolphins' Dan Marino.

From 1984 to 1986, Elway has led the Broncos to three of the four best seasons in their history. In that time, the Broncos won two divisional titles and an AFC championship.

In 1984, John led the Broncos to a 12-2 record. He finished eighth among AFC passers. An injured shoulder prevented him from starting in two games, although he was able to play for a time during each. The same injury kept him out of one game entirely. In a regular season game with the Vikings on November 18, John threw five scoring passes, tying the club's record for scoring passes in a single game.

Sacks are an occupational hazard for quarterbacks.

Fans ask their hero for autographs.

After the '84 season, John began working out in the weight room. He concentrated on building up his upper body and increasing his weight from its original 202 pounds. His new size and strength impressed his opponents. Although the Bronco handbook lists his weight at 212, Los Angeles Raider cornerback Lester Hayes maintains that "he's 220 if he's a pound."

In 1985, John "rewrote the Denver record book," as the club puts it, by setting five Bronco single-season records. He led the NFL with 605 attempts, which fell just four passes short of the all-time record held by Dan Fouts. He also led the NFL in total rushing and passing plays (656) and total offense (4,144 yards). He was second in the NFL in both completions and passing yards.

In 1986, his father noticed that John seemed confident, and that he was having a good time again. His confidence showed time and again in his performance. He started in all 16 games during the 1986 season. It seemed as though every time he turned around, he was breaking a record. Under his leadership, the Broncos went into the playoffs, captured the AFC championship and a spot in Super Bowl XXI.

John's passing arm is his most awesome offensive weapon.

IN THE PLAYOFFS

In the first playoff game, John and his teammates faced the New England Patriots. John sprained his left ankle during the first half and limped off the field at halftime. The score was tied 10-10. Coach Reeves wasn't sure John should go back into the game, but John wanted to try. He didn't come off the field until the game was over and the Broncos had won 22-17.

That win took the Broncos to the AFC Championship game against the Cleveland Browns, played at Cleveland Stadium. After a stunning catch by Cleveland wide receiver Brian Brennan, the Broncos were trailing the Browns 20-13 with 5 minutes and 32 seconds remaining in the game. Denver fans had thrown in the towel, and Cleveland fans were already celebrating the victory and the championship.

But in the words of baseball great Yogi Berra, "It's not over until it's over." For John, the game still had more than five minutes to go. His team was on their own two-yard line. In the huddle, John told his teammates, "If you work hard, good things are going to happen." He then marched the Broncos on a 15-play drive 98 yards down the field. With just 39 seconds remaining in the game, John threw a five-yard pass to Mark Jackson.

The pass found Jackson angling into the end zone and hit him hard. Touchdown! "I felt like a baseball catcher," said the 174-pound receiver. "That was a John Elway fastball, outside and low." As the clock ran out, the game was tied 20-20.

Strength, speed, and accuracy are necessary for any quarterback.

In overtime play, John was unstoppable. He lost no time in moving his team 60 yards, which gave Rich Karlis field goal position at the Cleveland 15-yard line. John told Karlis just before he kicked: "It's like practice." Karlis' field goal was good, and Denver beat Cleveland 23-20. The cheers of Bronco fans were loud and happy!

For John, success was mind over matter. Nothing stood in his way — not his bad ankle, not the cold and snowy weather, not the almost-certain defeat. "We shut him down the whole game," said Brown defensive end Sam Clancy, "and then in the last minutes he showed what he was made of."

John pivots to hand off to his running back.

Fading back, John searches for his receiver.

John and teammate Tom Jackson display the Broncos' AFC championship trophy.

Later in the locker room, Elway summed up his feelings about the game he had just played. "You know how you'll think, the night before, about how you'd like to do great things in the game? Well, this is the kind of game you dream about."

Their victory over Cleveland gave the Broncos the AFC Championship. The New York Giants had shut out the Washington Redskins 17-0 to win the NFC Championship. Two Sundays later, John and his teammates would face the Giants in Super Bowl XXI.

SUPER BOWL SUNDAY

The week before Super Bowl XXI, *Sports Illustrated, Time,* and *Newsweek* all ran articles about the upcoming game. Most experts thought the Giants would win by at least 10 points. They had performed strongly in their playoff games, overwhelming their two opponents. The Broncos, in their playoff games, had only squeaked through to win.

Yet some sports writers were still predicting a win for the underdog Broncos. "Being an underdog means nothing to us," said John before the game. "There's no pressure. We have everything to gain and nothing to lose."

Both John and Giant quarterback, Phil Simms, were at the top of their games in the 1986 season. And during the first half of the Super Bowl, they matched each other's performances. In fact, in the first quarter, neither quarterback threw an incompletion. By halftime, the Broncos had scored a field goal and a touchdown and were ahead 10-9. But their lead was shaky.

In the second half, the Giants changed their whole offensive attack and surprised the Broncos. Instead of relying on their strong running game, the Giants began to play a passing game. They scored four touchdowns and a field goal on their first five possessions in the second half. The Broncos lost, 39-20.

"We threw everything we had at them. I thought I did everything I could do," John said after the game. Despite

Ugh! Giants' players sack the quarterback at Super Bowl XXI.

his disappointment, he added, "The playoff games helped make me a better quarterback."

FOOTBALL AND FAMILY

John describes himself as "a private, fun-loving, family man." He and Janet live in a house atop a hill in Aurora, Colorado, a suburb of Denver. They have two daughters, Jessica Gwen, born in 1985, and Jordan Marie, born in 1987. Their family also includes a French poodle named Leroy and a black labrador named Rufus.

"I've been so fortunate," says John. "If I had to draw up a blueprint for life, it would be this." One more thing would also please him: to have a son with whom he could share his love of football, just like he did with his dad.

During the off-season, John is active in the Denver community. He is a member of the Mayor's Council on Physical Fitness and is Chairman of the National Kidney Foundation for the Rocky Mountain Region.

Early in 1987, John's picture was featured in three national newspapers in an ad about Denver. The ad was made to attract businesses to Denver. John was happy to cooperate. "I'm glad to be a part of anything that can help Denver," he said.

The Elways like living in Colorado. They have put down roots and really believe in the city and the state. Colorado likes the Elways, too. When John's five-year contract is up

To relax, John likes to play golf.

The Elway family.

John smiles easily and often.

at the end of the 1987 season, another contract with the Broncos will be waiting for him. The Denver Broncos and John Elway make a good team!

JOHN ELWAY'S PROFESSIONAL STATISTICS

YEAR (Starts)	ATT	COMP	YDS	PCT	TD	INT
1983 (10)	259	123	1,663	.475	7	14
1984 (14)	380	214	2,598	.563	18	15
1985 (16)	605	327	3,981	.540	22	23
1986 (16)	504	280	3,485	.556	19	13
CAREER TOTALS (56)	1,748	944	11,637	.540	65	64
POST-SEASON (4)	159	86	1,112	.541	5	7